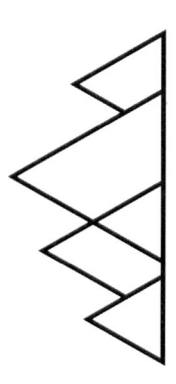

Soul & Machine

Wild Cat Nerd

Copyright © 2024 Soul & Machine, LLC.

ISBN: 978-1-7349036-5-2

For Florence & Miles,
Be good shepherds.

WILD CAT NERD

BY JUAN CARLOS

Yes, it's true. You must've heard.
I'm your friend, the wild cat nerd.
In rain or shine or on a train.
They're always, always on my brain.

SNOW LEOPARD

RUSTY-SPOTTED CAT

Now we're driving to the zoo,
going to see you know who.
Big cats, wild cats, giant and tiny.
Their oval eyes are bright and shiny.

At the entrance, we grab a map.
I point to lions, tap, tap, tap.
I circle all my favorite spots.
I'm the leader. I call the shots.

LION

CARACAL

Walking around the park and stalls,
I spot two small caracals.
Romping, rolling, double trouble,
there's another in the rumble!

Crouching low, the Ocelot
finds the perfect hiding spot.
Watching, waiting for its prey,
and suddenly, there's one to slay.

OCELOT

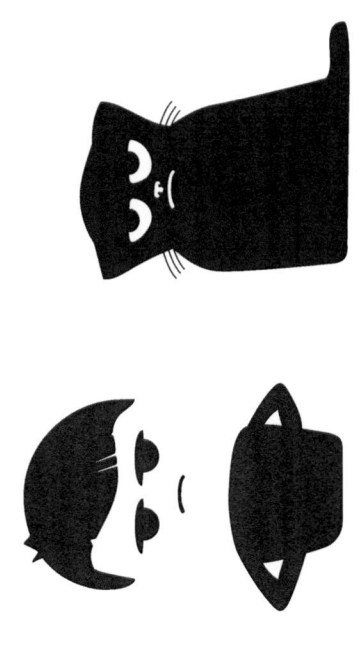

Manul pacing left to right.
Fur dark grey and snowy white.
Solitary, rarely seen,
this grumpy cat can be quite mean.

Bobcat roams, his senses heighten.
Could it sense a mountain lion?
A shadow, yes, nothing more,
but in the distance, hear a roar?

BOBCAT

MOUNTAIN LION

Bobcat hides for an hour

to avert a chance encounter.

But it was not long enough

Mountain Lion calls his bluff.

Hanging from a great big tree,
like a monkey, wild and free.
The clouded leopard is reversed,
climbing down a branch headfirst.

CLOUDED LEOPARD

JAGUAR

Now I'm hungry for a snack.

Popcorn in a paper sack.

While I'm munching, I miss the part,

where the jaguar lets out a fart.

Servals from Senegal.
Climbing walls so very tall.
The longest legs of any cat,
jumping high, nine feet at that.

SERVAL

SAND
CAT

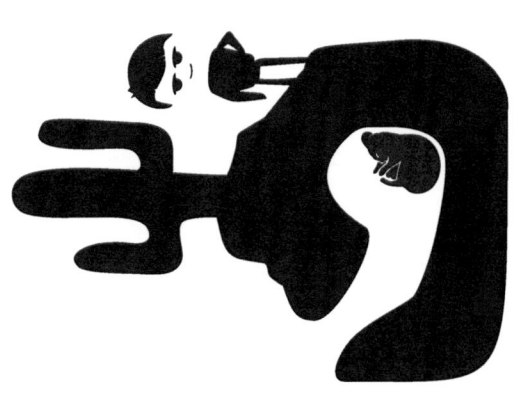

The sand cat burrows in the heat.

When it's hot, she cools her feet.

Hiding from the bright sunlight,

nocturnal creatures love the night.

A margay lives its life in trees,
sleeps in hollows, a tight squeeze.
Running, leaping, chasing birds,
he catches two and goes for thirds.

MARGAY

LEOPARD

Leopard spots are called rosettes,
a speckled coat to hide from threats.
In the forest's dappled light,
she conceals herself from sight.

Canadian Lynx prefer cold weather,
paws like snowshoes, tough as leather.
Enduring icy winds alone,
solo in the great unknown.

CANADIAN LYNX

EURASIAN LYNX

Eurasian lynx stalking, sneaking,
on high rocks scanning, seeking,
hungry for something sweet,
ambush a deer, a tasty treat.

The quickest animal on land,

Cheetahs' massive strides are grand.

Zero to eighty miles an hour,

fast and faster, sprinting power.

CHEETAH

BLACK PANTHER

From the shadows, a black panther

Jumps a boulder and launches after

A little mouse. Where did it come from?

Swallowed whole, the mouse is, umm... DEAD?

Tiger stripes are unique,
from their head to their feet.
Endangered species like no other,
we must treat them like a brother.

TIGER

ASIATIC
GOLDEN CAT

Going home from the zoo,
I say goodbye, feeling blue.
Waving to my wild cat friends,
Don't you worry, I'll be back again.

About the Author

Juan Carlos enjoys stargazing and watching agave americana trees bloom. He writes to help kids and adults be independent thinkers that make the world a better place.

Father to an amazing bird nerd and wild cat nerd. They live in the high desert, where they marvel at the world and the people in it.

While making this book, his daughter illustrated several cats. He is proud of her, but more importantly, she's proud of herself.